THE VISIBLE SPECTRUM

THE BOOK OF TREASURES
DUSTIN JUNKERT & SHANE MORITZ

The 54 poems in *The Book of Treasures* are the product of a longstanding collaboration. Shane Moritz and Dustin Junkert met in 2013 while attending graduate school at Georgia College & State University, where they fell into the habit of writing over each other's stories and poems as they passed the time in one of the town's few bars. At first it was an *If I were writing it, I'd probably say this…* type of thing—handwritten changes to printed drafts smudged with tzatziki. Although they owed allegiance to different literary schools, they tended to agree on the best punch lines, and wound up accepting each other's mocking overwrites often enough that they started to work together this way intentionally. It was amusing for each of them to hand over a draft and see what the other brought to it, until each piece eventually morphed into something for which neither was solely responsible. The final product became known as a *shanedunk* and the process as *dunking*—both terms coined by Professor of Poetry Laura Newbern, author of the much-admired collection *Love and the Eye.* Her influence rages here.

After grad school our heroes moved to different cities, but the dunking continued whenever they met up, in Boston, Philadelphia, Portland, Baltimore. Regardless of where they were written, their poems remain stamped with the spirit of the town in which their joint project was born— Milledgeville, Georgia, home of Flannery O'Connor. It was at her old homestead there—flush with peacocks and the barn from that one story still standing—that the first readings took place of versions of some of these poems.

As soon as they saw the illustrations David Nichols proposed for their poems, the authors were convinced ▶

▶that *The Book of Treasures* would not be complete without them; the melancholy vision expressed in his artwork draws out the tenderness underlying even their most unhinged scenarios.

DUSTIN JUNKERT was born in Tacoma, Washington, and now lives in Portland, Oregon, where he works in marketing. SHANE MORITZ was born in Portland, spent his formative years in Australia, and lives in Baltimore, where he teaches writing at the University of Maryland–Baltimore County. DAVID NICHOLS is a writer and artist who teaches urban history at the University of Melbourne; his most recent book is *Persiflage*, a graphic novel.

DUSTIN JUNKERT
SHANE MORITZ

The Book
of Treasures

POEMS

ILLUSTRATIONS BY DAVID NICHOLS

THE VISIBLE SPECTRUM

THE VISIBLE SPECTRUM SERIES 001

The Visible Spectrum Series is published by
Verse Chorus Press LLC, Portland, Oregon, USA
the-visible-spectrum.com

Text copyright © 2022 Dustin Junkert and Shane Moritz
Illustrations copyright © 2022 David Nichols

Cover and book design by Steve Connell | *steveconnell.net*

Cover illustration by David Nichols

ISBN 978-1-953835-01-7

Library of Congress Control Number: 2022931483

CONTENTS

THE BOOK OF TREASURES

THE HOP

The new town fit him like a sentence about an old shirt.
A death sentence about an old shirt.
She looked at him.
He thinks he's in his own mind, practically all the time.
She is crisp as a chip.
The drink, it was decided,
is what was making her feel sweet and mild.
That said, she switched to something else.
On the strength of her tutelage alone, he thought,
she could really get cooking.
He spoke now of a trend, of something to do overhead.
Flying — to fly.

She pointed out his misgivings.
He pointed out her foot.
She recalled the unbending light of an Egyptian dawn,
somehow edging away.
By lunch he had slipped into the pan of the gay Midwest,
then, in a sort of untimed hop, said his piece and you,
you believed in this man.
He had been walking in and out of his own funeral
his whole life long, it was said.
I made a commotion: saw stars, heard bells.
It is in this life, however, that a rodent-like yelp
can serve one only so well.

PRIMA FACIE

It's the act of providing descriptive detail
on top of allowing you to see her in the light
that plays most magnificently on her shoulder.

And this is coming from someone experiencing volleyball
from a distance, my frère.

Every day I walk myself into a state of mental elegance,
walking like there is much to celebrate.

The spring has a bedside manner we could learn from,
an air of rain-soakedness, a bouquet of crocuses,
a way to walk off my condition.

To live all the time is to live
in your avocado sweater!

My closet is an open book, a bobcat skull of autumnal import.
Don't ask me how some of this ethereal stuff gets out.

Cliché edits, oxblood cocktail, vainglorious tweeds
in herringbone gray for the evening blaze through the lamps.

I was nineteen and poorly groomed
with an indistinct future and a shrinking carrot
with a woodsy aroma.

A CIRCLE GATHERS AROUND A FALLEN DOPE

It's downright criminal,
the length of a weekend.
But give it time.
Get busy—things can get very
busy down at the hardware store,
but I don't have to tell you that.

You say something familiar,
and something similar to that,
something bad,
and make a startling discovery.
A certain deleting of dimensions.

Your generosity
has turned the cafe virtual,
converted the davenport into a bed
of frozen vegetables:
peas.

I have amnesia again!
And that's the good news.
The bad news?
The length of a weekend.

DRAGONFRUIT

Hello my sweet, I say.
I'd prefer not to.
In my palm, a dragon
of ripened fig.
She reaches for the moon.

Hello my fist, I say
over a breakfast toast.
In my face, orange juice,
all sorts of mayhem —
fruits of life hanging low.

I look at my then sweet
woman of the earth
through a door I painted.
Slice of life or not,
the knife keeps buttering.

LAND TRUST
to Paulina Jaeger

A man returns to his hometown one day.
Before long, he's seen occupying a ledge.

There's a folded scrap of paper on the bar.
An idiot's memoir: *I can't see a spot of air through the rush of rain.*
It's in cursive.

"What time is happy hour?"
"Every hour is happy hour."
"Is that true?"
"Everyday low prices."

My parents are completely at home in the living room.
I'm swishing ice around my glass
from inside the neighborhood gazebo
listening to an ancient party CD, when in walks a dear old friend.

We head over to the park and sit down in a place
where a few ants were having a picnic.
I was in a complete panic.

I could've been born at a whole different time, Paulina, I said.
A caterpillar inched over her hand,
impressively bridging the widening gaps between her fingers.
A little eternity passed there as we watched.

Something frightened us, a sound from the woods.
We stood up and peered around.
Kingdoms are built and razed from one moment to the next.

▷

I try to laugh but it hurts like hell
and all of a sudden I'm flooded with all the things I need
to do today to prepare for my trip to the Rockies.

AMERICAN REAL

I guard the art with museum dust
in my mouth and face. I see service dogs all the time
in languid isolation and it is my job to lose.

I am accompanied by an unending series
of masterpieces to comfort me, and my dogs
are obese, well-to-do gods.

Old women have such nice hands in a Hopper.
There's always an empty chair to be found.
Someone's in the coat check, undressing.

PICTURE THIS: A DOG

Out of the Crepuscular Fog,
by America's greatest painter since Oliver Sandstone.
A dog worn out of its own usefulness.
A dog living well beyond its means.
A dog, in a word, crepuscular, and absolutely shrouded in fog.
And what does he see?
A tawny lass sitting on a log
staring at a cloud.

What fur! Such ears!
What little credit I have, I afford to Oliver Sandstone.
O sassy after the sun sets mightily on this bog
might I find my lassie...
under the stars where the hours disrobe.

The crime scene of one's youth—
the blip of virtue—
the habit of holding... say, a muzzle in one hand,
a muzzleloader in the other.
Certain things get left behind.

MIKE AND MIRANDA

There once was a boy everyone liked named Mike.
Mike reclined next to a woodpile sometimes.
Once he lay down next to a postage stamp
of Marilyn Monroe in a bathing suit.

Miranda knew Mike, whose woodpile it was.
Sometimes Miranda lay down next to Mike,
after Mike had outgrown his clothes,
lying in a pile at his feet.

Day after day in the apple orchard
next to the woodpile, Mike
walked home
by what little light there was.

Once, Miranda looked Mike in the eye,
clouds circling his head like ravens.
They went to the orchard and the apples had fallen suddenly.
They turned to the orchard
and all the trees had been chopped down.

Sometimes Miranda lay down next to Mike . . .

GRAND CANYON

My friend was losing teeth and going blind.
I suggested we take a trip to the Grand Canyon
and produced the keys to an '89 Corvette.
He appears at first to be a large man,
but the closer I get, the smaller he gets.
He has the big glassy eyes of a doe
and sharp, kitten-like teeth, few as there are.

And like that we hit the road,
a few Ziplocs of sliced fruit in the glove box.
The shadows covered my eyes
except for hot blades of light that passed through my temples.
Juniper filled the air,
went up my mouth and nose and watered
the entertainment center of my eyes.

The ribs of an elk sat discarded beside the road,
a meat-covered birdcage the crows cleaned.
And what would it be like to be scavenged like that?
I had entered a primitive world with a blind guide.
He yawned and his few bottom teeth were like a little group
of white-hooded monks sneaking into a chasm.
I pulled over and we slept for almost five hours.

This is when the visions came.
We run straight down the switchbacks, arms akimbo.
Then I chip away at the underside of a wobbly boulder.
There's a perfectly fine-looking man
who I walk up to and shove with all my strength,
right over the edge, body shattering over the rocks.
The whole valley is nothing but an excuse for donkeys.

LYING

The person you see today is the one you'll see tomorrow,
and so on. From the grave to the sepulcher, have patience.
Control.
Have pivot foot.

I was preparing us to become men.
There is my father speaking again—
a stop sign uprooted in the sand.
The summer of alabaster—my summer, anyway.

When it seemed to me that you were on your way—
that is when I was poured an Irish bloodsport.
Not even very long ago, books contained the future, I was told,
a time of greatness now marked by blouses,

flying open like shutters in the haciendas of space and time.
In spite of a lifetime of daydreaming, you will resist
the tranquility of a rural life,
God knowing how that could go.

Now, a donkey incident:

The ass was straightforward and steadfast.
Like a boulder, to understand it required a brain wired
with more inner workings than the sum of the subject itself.
He meditates and thinks of both halcyon and terrible days.
He is communicating with me in his Catholic way,
Are social interactions happening here? Where?
A donkey dragging its feet—I'm like,
Every man you will ever meet, without exception, is lying
in a hammock on William Duffy's farm.

THE SCULPTURE GARDEN
to Annabel Bleach

Man does many excellent things in the sculpture garden.
Woos a local dogcatcher, broils rabbit,
and in some instances, has every notion to be outstanding.
One evening last March, man was not to everyone's taste,
neither over the road nor under the gazebo,
entering the sculpture garden in a dusty tuxedo
having thought himself to be the exception of a bath, little
choice but to anoint himself in various oils from the dogpatch.

My cravings for *douche* were, let me tell you, *nonpareil*.
I ensnared the dogcatcher in my nets.
I braised a bunny in the fire-encrusted swamp
and before the gates shut, smelt happy
as a fresh dug-up corpse.
I felt very free among the sun-dappled sculptures
and the sudden appearance of fighter jets in the sky.
They weren't there just to say hello either.

FATHER

My father, my god, a sun, clouds
zooming on the wind, saluting a sky full of nobodies,
a little shadow tracking fast over the ground.
I was the beneficiary of a rather large settlement
at an age I remember for how doggerel I was
by the mere desire to ask strangers
to go on.

Yesterday somebody's kid
wandering the aisles repeatedly:
time well spent at the Cineplex.
I wake to find a man in a dark suit
sitting on my bed with a wide-eyed cat in his lap.
It did not take long to see.
"Take what you want," I cried.

RUN-OF-THE-MILL LEGEND

A man eats soup with a ho-hum hand.
From the balcony his grandmother tries to stand.
Someone walks into a room—a panther seizes a stag forever.

Our eyes meeting like camels across a trough.
The lavender light veers downward, ripping into the hill.
In the silence, a pebble drops into a clear pool.

"I don't want to have to eat half a hot dog out in the rain,"
you report, but sadly.
This is precisely the sort of problem I know.

On my bike I crash into a snake.
The girl who I tell a block up the street shrugs.

The panel approves

THE IDEA

A young man has an idea.
He presents it to a panel.
The panel approves.

There is a frightful incident.
A young man enters the street
swaddled in a shower curtain.

The idea is replaced
by a list of household chores.
The panel approves.

Some fool the eye.
And others just fool the needle.
That is your tip for today.

SPRING

From my origins
in ice cream parlors around the world
to my rejection of all
foundations of thought.

The prince of the moment
has arrived.
Wanna feel old?
The Maltese Falcon.

My mama,
my Spring,
nary a solitary thought,
salons around the world.

Hey, why the distaste?
Why bullying around?
I chomp baking soda
for the teeth.

You will proceed into a state
where you're protected by
guards who won't bless you
even in the face of a sneeze.

PUT YOUR BEST BOOT FORWARD

Falling off my horse and dropping several stories
in a matter of seconds due to the horse standing on the top edge
of an apartment complex where I found it
is now how I picture my day going.
I'll pause to observe whatever the view affords
during the voyage down, the modest sprawls of domestic decency
bursting forth from the windows, gilded mugs half-full
posing beneath a cattywampus Hills Hoist of fluttering underwear,
a few Adirondacks abandoned at queer angles—
the image of this frozen moment seeming to bend
over the windowsill to follow my descent
the way old light skirts a planet so you can almost see
right through what's standing in your way.
This is the way of lusty men, and there is something to be said
for the cowhand who picks his horse out with conviction.

MARYLAND HEALTH CLUB

Cloistered among the ellipticals,
nuns climb the walls
to build their modest calves.
Some Greek and Roman sculptures
make their hay around the free-weights,
their bronze calves
apocalyptic with muscularity.
Whatever that exercise is,
it looks miserable, and I lose it.
Apollo drinks at the fountain.
The water is ice cold and he makes
audible wishes between gulps.
Party music engages as a new shift begins.
The nuns and I climb the stair
to the convalescent home.
I have turned my back
on everyone I ever loved.

III

Construction

BEASTIE

You spot your doppelganger on the beach
skipping waves,
not appearing to be in any real danger,
if he's anything like you.
How similar we all look to one another,
from a certain distance.

You were washed up, crushed by other people's dishes,
a bona fide product of the service industry.
Which is to say: food. You would get eaten alive.
The water was immensely cold,
even as it blasted out of the faucet this was apparent.
Was there ever a moment this small?

The fog wore your clothes
and cleaned your teeth
and watched your shows and showed up
at your job and carried your luggage.
At the altar, you are mistaken for your baby brother
and baptized wearing a tarpaulin sheet
in the secretary's jacuzzi.

It's now years earlier.
You turn up in the living room
and in the frozen silence the room is exploding,
the furniture tumbling backward before
your mother turns to you.
She wipes the cobwebs from your hair.

VOCATION

Look there, the train is rolling right out of the station without us.
Nothing but pink clouds for miles and the next train
leaves in a year.
I suppose it's back to the yard then.

Before long, we'll be wrecking the bamboo shoots,
the same ones we handled all year
like the smooth, delicate arms of babies —
you just want to graze your cheek against them sometimes.

Reaching for the sun isn't the worst impulse —
plenty of plants do something of the sort. Anyhow,
what we'll do to the bamboo shoots next is not for babies.

Let's go back inside, put on some incense, and swallow knives.
The kind of thing that as soon as you do it once, you ask yourself,
why on earth don't I do this every day?

And then you go and never do it again,
until maybe you have company.
But we don't get a whole lot of company.
You can thank the train schedule for that.

Look there, the train is rolling right out of the station without us

THIS LITTLE SUBURBAN LIFE OF MINE

My struggles, my elongated chest.
The mule wearing my shoes in a paddock beside the grocer.
Or the goat staring at a root from across the moat.
Out on the country road you shed clothes for a Speedo.
I fall asleep under a tree.
A spiky, inked woman in a vest: Charli pulls over.
Charli is what was made from what seemed to be the right way
to weather a storm to two blue and comfortless people.
It is a short taxi home to the inevitable.
In your hand, the apocalypse in the form of a sandwich.
You manipulate her vote as the woman takes the whopper.
Trompe l'oeil for scenery, mild undulations, learning centers.
To climb these walls—it is her wish, she says—
and to open an antique store somewhere behind them.

It is a funeral: that is the destination.
There is something to be learned about the family tree
even while it is being blown to smithereens.
Funeral notes: He drives a car into an automotive center,
right into the front door, through the glass and everything.
He makes a small environmental footprint, otherwise.
He makes a dent in a cul-de-sac in the low outskirts.
There's a cigar warming in the microwave.
He has more where that came from.
A battle at the HOA meeting, before all this:
"I hope you are not questioning my husband's integrity," she says,
"He is an honest man, and an earnest man."
You say, "My father's name is Ernest."

REBRANDING

Get me a clawfoot and a headlamp
and I'm happy as a clam.
I forge steel four nights a week.
The feeling of bathing is like I am the awakening dog
under a specific neighborhood curfew.
Off I go then, into the feral woods.
You call that exercise?
One morning my mother furnished me
with a simple Amaro.
I went to work a new man that day,
or a new dog, if you like,
with a replenished doggy bowl
full to the brim with puppy chow.
Overflowing, in fact.
The guys at work bopping around
in their asbestos suits
pulling hot molds from the oven.
Foreman Allen and his twisted tales
of ghost pepper poppers.
You call this a refinery?
From the belly of a ripped glove
I bulged a bare knuckle against the wheel
of the stand grinder—totally improvised.
I'm staring at an exposed tendon,
wondering if I'll have to ask to get my check.
A megamillionaire with an SLR stands beneath the archway
wearing a sarcoline *chemisier*.
That is, a flesh-colored blouse.
It is the advertiser.

THE STORY OF MAN

On the side of the mountain you felt a stitch in the lumbar
pining for the vortex.
At a switchback you upended your mix
and met a man who offered to fix your back.
A family of four came down from the cold, crimson and bored.
The light of the afternoon faltered under sudden weather.
There are issues regarding the curvature of your spine,
the man told you, and opened his valise
to rummage through a pile of tools.
The wind howled through the trees.
The man leaned back and reminded himself
where his beard was and its contours.
He considered which journal to publish your case in. You waited...
He asks you to remove all your clothes.
Strictly procedural, he says.
You step behind a shrub to comply.
The wind wraps around your back,
which had been hurting.
The man draws from an odorless spliff
and directs you to walk in a line,
pivot on a heel, and touch your toes.
A sound coming from the switchback:
a considerable gathering, with horns, gongs.
A deep floor tom: ominous.
A funeral march?
"Seems like one happens nearly every day," he says,
"and the whole town is in attendance sometimes."
You rest your hands on your hips and a light sprinkle commences.
Picture rain glancing off the brass instruments.
Everything is here except a pocket to put it in.
You turn to see the man rattle down the switchback for town,
the rain ribboning through what's left.

THE RECOVERY HOSPITAL

I've thought about the oddity of the number zero—
one thinks of many things, over time.
I, in futility, happenstance a snifter.
What use have I for this, being the opposite of an early adopter?
I am in many ways a laggard in matters of the nose.
I feel like an overturned bus with a man or two still inside.
And who will be the first responder in this situation?

Sheila—I like her, in spite of the trouble.
I gravitate toward her gurney.
I point to a static aspen, through the window.
"*Populus tremulus*," she says royally.
"The tremors of the people," I add.
"You may go now," she says, as two flies gather on her toes.
I felt like a cat who had found a thin ledge.

I toted a sledgehammer around, the weekdays.
Plant 5 was my *bête noire*.
The main plant was on 23rd and Vaughn, but my duties
befell a real blast zone—over the B-side of the dunes.
I fell asleep in heat.
The shrinking day—I'll never get used to it.
And what about that smell? Some calcified screwiness.

Another visit to the recovery hospital.
Sheila is much different now: she is in love—
she says that she is in love with me.
This happens now and again.
The clouds move in, passing shadows over the grass.
A breeze pushes everything slightly one way.
Then again I was released, somehow, from my obligation.

THE SKYSCRAPER

He was an important man to many—such as his parrot, Rusty.
And to others, he was a portly man—not unlike his dog, Rusty.
He had fled the war at one point and gone north
to join a wrecking crew. Using modern methods,
and with the help of his crew, he could bring a skyscraper
straight down over its own foundation,
with nothing for collateral but a whiff of dust.
And what is a man without his wrecking crew?
A wreck—that is the answer.

My grandfather met a lady
who filled many roles for people in society.
She was the Minister of Education,
and she became his wife on top of it—the skyscraper, that is.
The wedding was a crew job,
taking place at five hundred feet
against the top railing of a condemned dance hall.
Maurice, the masonry tech, practiced a few jokes
meant to link the sentiments of marriage and demolition:
a calculation that resulted in the construction of my family.

"How was work?" the parrot, Rusty, inquired.
"An absolute disaster," my grandfather said.
He crashed onto the couch in a well-lit part of the room.
Rusty licked his hand, the dog did.
My grandfather slipped to the floor,
being a young man at this point,
and placed his hat in his hand, as the dog broke for the door.
"I'm having a bad day," he said.
"Same," said Rusty.

DOMESTIC INTERIOR

I was an excitement,
girdled by tungsten.
You leaned on a hot-rod prototype,
smudging up the side.
We zipped around.
The future: imagine!

Your parents put up
an eerie sauna in the basement.
A gathering place for woodland creatures.
Used as often as you would imagine.
Perhaps we were meant to die
in somebody else's socks.

There is a coziness to one version of the future.
You sit in a nasty chair
waving your nasty hair.
Then I go down to the place
where a grubby animal
suffices on sins.

THE NAMELESS

Remember the time I surrounded you?
I almost got sick that day, or at least called in sick.
The situation is now this: danger.
Insouciance, my foot.

One day our family pet, the aptly named Bun-Bun,
gave birth to a litter under cover of dark.
In the morning we found Bun-Bun solitarium,
vermillion eyes, abutted with blood and bones.

So much happens in the six o'clock hour.
It is later than you would think.
"Someday I'll emerge," I think on innumerable occasions.
Emerge like a Phoenix, or a Flagstaff. A Tombstone.

"What's wrong with your foot?" I said,
and you assumed a pose beyond presumption.
Now that I'm older and draped in clothes,
I'm left with this business of that other life.

Names seem to mutate, adapt to circumstances.
Doors are entered and exited willy-nilly.
What use have I for a watch—
it is noon from where I'm standing.

The streets are peopled with crabs—
scuttling into their broilers.
I lie on the hot iron roof of my bungalow
seared by crop-dusters angling low.

THE POLICEMEN'S BALL

I went to the policemen's ball as a horse.
It is enviable to leave the house with a newspaper
over one's face. In my dirty overcoat
I carried my horseshoes through to the back room.
In the kitchen a typist stopped me,
hoping to gain perspective on a dessert
that harbored some elusive quality. I sampled a forkful
and paused significantly with a finger raised.
I said, "A mellow compote elegy."
She nodded and scribbled on a small blackboard.
I added, "And that is coming straight from the horse's mouth."

The final room of my tour came into view.
There I shook hands with a considerable gathering of officers.
Two more entered carrying in a folded card table
which manifested like a beach umbrella thrown open.
The first hand was dealt. I have them fooled.
This is not what I said, but what I thought.
I slotted a handsome club into the fold
that I had fished from my cuff as I ponied up.
The stakes? Of course I knew—
I was a quiet, plodding workhorse
and there was much work to be done.

One policeman took a long swallow of a Yankee Doodle.
Another stood against the far wall,
reaching two fingers down her throat
to retrieve her next hand.
There's a long pause as we all piece together
that no one's playing an honest game.

It is now time for a tale of destruction:
the other characters it concerns
figure into the ending as trampled.
What if I were to wrap my arms
around a memory such as this, and then fold?

I went to the policemen's ball as a horse

IV

The Agency

THE DISAPPEARANCE OF AGNES

It's about three o'clock.
There's a clutch of paperwork to do, but the person who does it
has gone missing. Maybe she's having a surreptitious delivery,
or her van disappeared under a bale of hay.
I do what any sensible man would do:
I dispense a craven menthol,
consult my copy of *Foxe's Book of Martyrs*, and make way.
There's Draco, the ancient legislator,
whose thankful supporters tossed so many hats,
cloaks, and shirts onto him that he suffocated and died.
In 1903, someone was beaten to death with a Bible
during a healing ceremony in Honolulu.
Another tale to prove that anything is possible,
watching the day wind down over here,
a view of the abattoir falling over into the riverbed.
Oh, Agnes. I read on.
In 1974, Basil Brown, a 48-year-old health food advocate
died from liver damage after he consumed
70 million servings of Vitamin A
and around ten gallons of carrot juice in ten days,
turning his skin the wrong color.
One year later, a man named Alex Mitchell laughed
for 25 minutes straight before falling dead
on top of a whoopee cushion.
Aeschylus, it says here, was killed by a tortoise
dropped by an eagle that had mistaken Aeschylus's bald head
for a rock suitable to shatter the shell of the reptile.
Who will complete the paperwork?
She stopped coming in six days ago now.
It's not a terribly efficient office.

▶

Late in the afternoon, next day, I am on my way to a haircut
when I resolve to go back to the office
and remove Agnes from payroll.
As I'm poring over my desktop for the link, Agnes walks in.
She had requested the time off, I'm told.
I look in my diary—it's true.
On the other side of the office, my colleagues
are shooting quarters across the table into each other's fists,
bloodying themselves rapidly.

THE TIME I MET A MAN ON THE BUS

One day I met a man on the bus on the way to the beach.
He had a bump on his head.
"How did you get that bump on your head," I said.
How he replied surprised me.
It was as if he had answered the phone
and couldn't hear who was on the other end.
"Hello... Hello?"
"Hi," I said. Could he be blind?
I waved.
He waved back.
That was all for now, and I was happy
to square back up in my seat and look at the scenery awhile.
The bus ride lasted ages.
The man with the bump returned to me.
He told me he liked to ride a BMX.
To my surprise, I got to see this.
We got off at his stop.
I was a long way from the beach, swirling a cup of brew.
Imagine me nodding my head
as an old two-wheeler faithfully circles
a backyard dirt track walled in by brambles.
He's late for dinner.
A perfect time for me to leave, in retrospect.
But it's been weeks now—
me in this spacious attic with a fresh pair of unfamiliar clothes
placed at the foot of my bed
morning after morning.

THE COLONEL

There are some renovations to do before I can rest:
install a freezer box in the corner,
construct an island to makes sense out of the kitchen,
build out a spare room off to the side.
I want to create accommodations for my new friend, the Colonel.
I met him on the floor of Jerry's Tavern,
where he was rolling batteries down his arm,
and I wound up putting him up for the night.
The next morning the Colonel fractured his femur fixing an omelet,
one in a series of injuries he suffered under my care,
only slightly dampening his otherwise incorrigible spirit.
He likes to get involved at dinner parties.
At a certain point in the evening, he tends to have a toast prepared,
angled toward who the guest seemed to him to be at first glance.
Annie came over once wearing a blush trench coat
and the Colonel hardly waited until the pouring of coffee
to recite the Hippocratic Oath for her. It didn't land.
A little while later, the Colonel, still feeling obliged to entertain,
said, "I'm going to show you how to take a fall."
"Please don't do that," she said.
Shortly after this, she noticed how late it had gotten.
The Colonel gave a deep bow as Annie left,
and all manner of well-wishes, then he settled into an armchair,
dislocating his shoulder. If I had his little room built out by now,
it wouldn't be such trouble—his recovery times are escalating.
Against my advisement, he went out for a walk this morning
and I do not know when I should expect to see him again.
I'd like to get a frame in place and maybe
one wall sheet-rocked by the time he returns.

THE BOTTOM LINE

Throughout the whole business of listening to this guy
try to explain his confused genius,
not once did I acknowledge
any uncomfortable feeling in my nether regions.
And not for lack of trying.
I raised my hand at first,
then gradually began waving it side to side.
But for whatever reason my hand was not called on.
Once I even reached up higher than I was previously able,
strangely surging out of my seat.
But this made little difference.
Instead, over and over again, the guy pointed at other hands.
Meanwhile, there was mine, waggling urgently.
When I saw him chuckle a little bit once,
at something someone said, I thought,
I will make that chuckle sound forced by comparison.
Or, if I choose not to get a laugh,
in the event that I do ever get called on—
a dear wish of mine, I assure you—
then perhaps I will bring a tear to your eye instead.
What a poignant moment that will be.
And this might be the right path,
as it sidesteps the aspect of competition altogether.
Then it's no longer a question of whether the dude
will enjoy my comment more than someone else's.
Instead, my comment will be of an entirely different order,
such that a comparison simply couldn't be made.
In fact, that's a certainty,
because what I had to say during this episode in my life,
and quite a few others as well,
wasn't a matter of choice, but of necessity.

Truth be told, there was only ever one thing I had to say,
if my moment came.
And what I wanted to express
is that it hurt down there—
in the bottom especially.

PLANNING A DINNER IN THE VILLAGE

You decide to distill the whole of a life into a dinner
you were to organize, split into a throng of tight courses,
each with its own set of silverware.
The menu itself undergoes extensive rewrites,
in light of changes in seasonal offerings
on which previous drafts relied.
You assemble the guest list to contain names
from every phase of your life: middle school,
construction, and up to the agency.
You are excited, clearly, yet at the same time,
going out of your mind.
The sleepy cottage you settled into
seems almost incapable of holding any amount of light.
A candle would be swallowed whole the moment a flame flicked,
although the assurance of sleep in such a climate
did something to settle the mind.
It is here that the real plans simmered, while you slept:
plates coupling as naturally as droplets on a window.
Upon waking, you scribbled down all you could remember,
grasping at the contours of incredible entrées,
just as they dissolve into the morning air,
careful to dismiss dishes which were actually fantastical
and contained impossible ingredients.
The afternoon was a time for sketches,
adding the new courses to observe
how they alter the overall effect.
The neighbors are increasingly curious about your room,
and they seek opportunities
to peek into the windows while you're away.
You must shoo them off,
even sometimes from within the room.

▶

All this is tiring work, but the evenings are quiet.
This is the program, more or less,
as the days ticked toward the happy event.
One night you are awakened by the scratch of tiny claws.
With no hope of light penetrating the room,
you are left to trudge around as if under a blanket
in search of the sound.
This effort, you have already guessed, leads to nothing.
The noises continue.
The next night you entertain a history of friends
at the long-awaited dinner, and compliments follow you
regarding the meticulous preparations . . .
This, of course, is a dream
from which you wake in a pool of bed-wet,
for lack of a better term.
The next morning the stains are visible from the street.

BABYLON

You are inspired by rust.
You are prone to spells of unconscious bleakness.
You have old hair.

You return from vacation with a door key
that reads *Key to the Rockies.*
You found it in a bush, brushed with rust.

Rust is the key, you tell Judy.
It's on the key, from one point of view,
and it is the key itself, from another.

Occasionally at the office you get called a name
you don't hear every day—a pejorative.
Your image appears in a mirror, lost behind a potted plant.

You loved three things in life:
Don McLean, green-headed ducks,
and bathymetric maps.

There's a company party at the aquarium.
You're able to carry around a newt, as a gimmick of the event.
The newt is a wild orange with some blue spots on its head.

You hold the newt in one hand, a negroni in the other.
"What exactly is it that you do again?"
Relief is coming, but in an unfamiliar form.

▶

"I shouldn't say," Judy says.
She looks spellbound by the creature on the table,
which is running volatile laps around the clam dip.

Yesterday I woke up a moth.
How sad! I said, and fled for the keyhole.

MY WEDDING DAY

One year later, I decide to jump a train
to another part of the country.
Then, as I have been told, I dropped to the cold
concrete surface of the factory.
I had to walk myself to my own alkaline.

You were a fruitful acquisition,
garnering considerable intelligence
from some known people —
brilliant minds, winners of prizes.
To your credit, all along you were asking at what cost.

Again, the great commute set you off
on a crooked orbit.
I had none to eat of Ms. Bean's berries,
as you had overturned the tables
by the time I thought to reach out for them.

Honeymoon at the Inn of the First Tamale:
bed and breakfast.
Getting matching facelifts
in a Tex-Mex municipality.
Next door, the strip club sells tumbleweeds on plaques.

YOUR WEDDING

Sit me down next to somebody absolutely frigid
and I will be quite at home at your wedding.
I will not subject the narrative to that.
For the love of god, the cold of night, and now a suit
hung over my shoulders before an ad hoc duck pond.

This would be the back nine of the month, year of our lord.
Majority of the buildup I witness from a folding chair
where one dutiful server brings me a reposado on a tiny platter
that sends swords of light through the wedding party
tightly clustered around a magnificent photographer.

I rarely put myself in situations these days.
Down by the pond a couple boys
cautiously pick something out of the sand.
A maimed seagull? A length of driftwood?
Perhaps I am the man-to-be.

A bridesmaid passes holding a cell phone to her head,
an expression of deep concern issuing sumptuous lines
across her brow. She appears to be someone
no one on god's green earth could get a chance to talk to.
Suddenly I get called a name you don't hear every day: Mister.

My lone ally has once again approached in my time of need
with a single, silent, diaphanous blanco.
The guests are finally filling in the gaps around me
and all at once that music starts with not a cloud in the sky.
I'm grinning wildly, aren't we all?

I rarely put myself in situations these days

MY WIFE HAS TWO GRAZED KNEES

I had been looking for someone,
out of cities and into a construction site, a Xanadu of latticework.
You tend to your knees
the way a turtle tends to the sand.
Fortunately I'm applying for a research grant
in treating minor cuts and abrasions.

In some instances, the chattering of ice
may be the thing to stave off what was coming for another day.
For now, I have applied iodine
in an ochre trickle over the shin,
thumbing it down in the fudge of dark,
my abs sore from fire.

V

Reconstruction

THERE, THERE

I was feeling like a leper,
so I held a religious congregation at my house.
As the celebration continued into the night,
a guy came over. I didn't know him.
He told me he was a hermit.
Later I found him asleep in the closet.
I said, "Jerry?"
He pulled his cap down over his eyes.
"Is that you, Jerry?"
"Yes, this is the captain speaking," he said.

But I'll be back at the office soon.
Or the swamp.
A memo landing on my desk,
fat with portent.
A bag of erasers for my birthday.
A satanic spreadsheet.
There is the feeling sometimes of the old
target on the head.
And you keep on going because it's
this way or that, so.

Scrounging after bits of paper is the plan
until one day you control half the room.
Who would like to see me again in this condition?
I was not unlucky once.
But there is no time for a memory.
There was little else for me to do
but watch volleyball at the beach.
Bring your Bible out there.
The songs aren't bad.
Why don't you say something, dear?

SOMETIME WEST OF THERE

But I halt this moment
in order to give in to a type of inertia
the elderly famously employ.
No reason to believe
I should have been in first yet.
It was as if they had seen me before,
somewhere on the internet,
taking apart a plot
for even greater profit.
In all toil there is reward, even if it ends in abasement.
And that's the Bible.
Inside the auditorium I discover a storm of wind
offset by occasional stalks of calm.
The mind reels at the things people will say
when surrounded by virtual assistance.
Help me find someone.
A lord. A heritage person.
To bed! For tomorrow we rise.
We must pray to come unglued.
I'll be the first to leave town if this is appropriate,
but I think you're going to like it.

HOME RUN

Things have been good in several ways.
You can't make a horse turn around midstream,
but you don't have to lead it to water either.
I had the desire to revisit a more innocent time,
in a sweater charged up like a bug-zapper.
An entity emerged through the business of dust and flies—
someone you trust. Someone's dad?
This man on a horse offered to take us down the gorge.
I asked him, before the lantern was lit,
about the olden days.
He met me with endless silence.
And now the lantern flickers on,
revealing telling glimpses of the fjord.
And what about that flamboyance I recall having?
I need to sit down, I tell our guide, feeling ill.
In small ways, you place your life in the hands of others.
In some of those old cavalry battles, did the horses
grasp the historical significance, do you think?
Or was it just another matter of beating the hooves awhile?
Trying out excuses, I appealed to our guide.
Could we *possibly* proceed, given the circumstances?
His reply was as terrible as it was inevitable:
that it was my call.

EXCELLENT INCORPORATE

I'll start an email with the application of just force
in the rococo style through the use of propped mirrors
which, not unlike us, are describing each other incompletely.
A view from the window. A smidge or two.
The downside of a literary affliction is taken at face value.
In the yard, cowbells usher in evening.
But, god, how good are things at the office,
holding your breath, praying?
A mantis holding his head against a beet cabbage.
In the window is a face scribbled with memos.
Somebody else will have a revolution and the answer for it.
You're well read. There is a haunted platform in your head.
Where is the heart? To find, search within formulas.
I've got a sizeable expenditure of pâté on my plate.
We each have one, to promote wellness.
I'm all well fed now, but not at all well.
There is a character in one cell refusing to be counted.

EULOGY

He was a good and brave man
who I'd aspire
to support to his grave,
as his attorney.
Whatever incidents
he endeavored pursuant to
and including his death
were circumstantial,
simple, and pure.

He sent me to his tailor
who measured
and made me
shirts of silk.
I wore Bulgarian cologne
on his charge.
My topsiders were equal
to any in town,
thanks to him.

Yet I find myself
in need of encouragement
on this day,
brooding on the question
of whether beauty
can be made,
or only found.
How two eyes can fix
on one object.

When I was young I used to sit on the riverbanks

TACOMA IN THE AFTERNOON

When I was young I used to sit on the riverbanks
watching *Spawn*.

Frivolous afternoons waylaid in June,
the water rippling out like diced onions.

I almost said something once to this beautiful man
who I supposed to be in a kind of stupor.

The nurse was complaining about youth
in a remote fishing village in Tacoma.

The man winced and said, Nurse,
to be fair I have it worse.

IN THE REALM OF IGNITION

I attend a continuing education class with my buttocks clenched.
My associates are philistines.
We have long chats about theft, and motorcycles.
The words I speak are somehow ground down,
as if filtered through a bag.
I am no good with names.
My opinions are made of dust.
The instructor had been awarded a Pulitzer
for coverage of the Mount Saint Helens eruption in 1980.
It was my own research that taught me this, not him—
which made the fact palatable.
There was this party, a few months in.
It took an hour for anyone to risk the wine.
My heart was a river in the desert.
There is a ship to be taken, my instructor told me privately.
Some people think God resides in the lake.
Others think God lives in special collections.

VI

Cow Herding Pictures

JOIN THE CLERGY

I coasted along the highway under a bolt of lightning.
Normality: the primary goal for the day.
Under a rain shelter I ran into a harlot
who made several rational arguments
that led me to a place where she and I would be purified.
It was the local abbey,
and I was drying off by the time we hit the steps.
Sitting on a rock near the rail, a trollop waved.
I entered the chapel, and was offered a draconian beer.
Outside, the sky was tender and clear—
I could see it through the windows behind the monks
who were wiping their brows on their thick brown sleeves.
Above the roof is hell on earth.
Things are tearing our lives apart.
The stuff of leisure is unseemly.
Even the wolves will one day be held to task.

HOW TO TEACH A CANARY TO SING

You are unemployable,
which means you get to wheel your cart out and get all over town.
You are here in the tender afternoon
discovering the joy in the simple things
as people start leaving in bunches.
Wave to the kid outside the barber shop eating a candy cane.
"Hey kid, cool crewcut!"
He freezes as if he was seeing a ghost.
A salamander stops you in front of the condemned IHOP.
You look at its face—could that be a smile?
In the forgotten city, you are a few beers short of a keg.
You see a doctor hurrying across the street.
"Hey doc, what's wrong with my neck?"
The doctor ducks, to show that he has heard you,
then stumbles and loses his cap altogether.
What a man!
Yesterday there were loons out here—
an old construction site where the builders got a better idea—
probably went off to find
a new cup of tea to match the great liberty of the soul.
You rest your body that aches in every conceivable way
next to a red barn. Here you will wait.
Soon someone comes—it's a man—this should be interesting.
He looks nonplussed even as he ages rapidly.
He shows you what he's got: a record
entitled, "How to Teach a Canary to Sing."
He whistles a long sonorous tune, it is difficult to follow.
Another visitor:
you bemoan what is sure to be a diversion—
by all accounts a salesman.

▶

He explains that the sky is colorless
while the barn is totally unsaturated.
After a turbulent somatic negotiation,
you accompany him to the cool damp of the barn.
But the world has changed.
You see that tree?
The day someone asks you where you are
will be a difficult one.

HOW TO APPROACH A MAN FROM WITHIN A BOX

Enter and leave your bed at the same time each day.
Soothe the man from its wilderness
by a ritual of behavior as invariable as its own.
Divert the glare of the eyes, hide the tremor of the hands,
shade the brilliantly reflecting face, the mighty smile.
Assume the stillness of a tree.
A man fears nothing he can see clearly and far off.
That is worth remembering.
Approach him across open ground
with steady, unfaltering movements.
Let your shape grow steadily in size but do not alter its outline.
Never hide yourself unless concealment is complete.
Be alone, as circumstances allow.
Shun the furtive oddity of man, cringe from the hostile eyes
of street cats and other creatures who may happen to be around:
small bugs, scraps of paper.
Learn to fear.
To share fear is the greatest bond of all.
Each moment of one's life
must have the quivering intensity of an arrow thudding into a tree.
Yesterday is a dim monochrome.
A week ago, in a way, you were not born.

A man fears nothing he can see clearly and far off

A MAN IS GOOD TO FIND

Let's have a drink.
Follow me to Kentucky
my ass.

You make a series of gestures
and your suit fits your shoulders
like safari fruit.

In the bowels of my many excellent years,
one by one my big boots
come off like a grape.

These nights have a satisfied sense,
the air thick with office ridicule
and purses begging for emptiness.

What did you do with the nymph?
Where did she go?
Suddenly her feet were poised for the cantina.

LOVE IN THE INSTITUTE

I get put in here all the time for losing my marbles.
See this? One of many in a swift arsenal.
Just when you think I am about to submit, a clamp comes down.

And when you think I am thinking about something germane...
I lean forward to perish with absolute contentment
on the recreation floor.
Can I trouble you for a glass of sinkwater?

At the breakfast table, I had ice for veins.
A new inmate arrived, outfitted in a malignant smock
in the befitting glare of the full afternoon.

She explains that the hemispheres of her body
do not have the temerity to handle an anachronistic moment,
much less the present one.

I get strange dreams like
I am driving down an icy boulevard, I tell her.
Nights: concubines
clattering outside my window around the maypole.
I extend my hand.

A stilted laugh comes from a jumpy man
in the other room—an employee.
Right when I wish someone would catapult me into the glass,
someone does. I had gotten a letter from his mother:

"Dear sir, I do hope you are getting on well.
I pray the facilities are normal and functional."
This was not her last letter. We jump into a love affair that reeks.

BOOK OF TREASURES

I trampled the earth until I found a spot that took.
There was enough of a backlog that I could be illustrating shrubs
for days. Backbreaking labor seemed to be the only outcome
when things took their natural course.

The neighbor is coughing up again, striving for some form
in this life, passing by one window, then another.
"Why don't you eat something?" I hear a woman say.
A grin and a smile as the lamb with little wolf eyes agrees.

I, for one, have given up on faces, them insane visions.
A mythical version of the town is with us,
settled silently among the streets.
Every so often you wind up on one.

We got here early to find that all the chairs were gone.
The lesson in this can be hard to see.
The candy is bountiful in the shops you ransack in your sleep.
The county has ordered a recall on all fiat currency.

LOST AT SEA 2

O be alive with the wind,
wherever
this is.

A boy drinks
a screwdriver on the prow.
He has a plank
in his eye.

Garçon,
the sky is retiring—
I know you know that—
I suggest
you do the same.

The yardarm creaked as he dozed in the dusk.
I can hardly see.

And I sing
a cappella to all thee
assholes
lost at sea—
and when
I die,
recalled in jeans,
smashed by a yardarm,
as is my fear,
I let
the mist
meet me.

▶

Look at me, I seem to be
full as the moon.

MYTH SLEAZE

The refrigerator is empty
and all the guests
have gone home.
Rest of the year
contains no plan
and what lies before me
by turns delectable
divorced now
from my potpourri,
each day detectable
by smell alone.
It is a lurid moment
of thought-making.
Yet the animal roams.
It is I,
facing the corner,
perched on a stool,
defending my inches,
submitting an application
for entry into the cosmos.
The animal—a dog—
goes around barfing up
a storm.
I can smell it.

DINING TWICE FOR MY 44TH BIRTHDAY

This TV dinner cooling on the windowsill—
enough for a still life. A guru in Pilates once told me
to rotate my ankles before bed
as an ancient protection against modernity.
O, how they saw it coming.

I lost some guts to a man who promised me
a Glen Campbell song at my funeral.
Aren't we all assailed by a Milledgeville madman?
It is you, death, the archivist, approaching me in the drift.

The desert—martial, crude.
The sun and its gold watch—it is 10 am,
and you dip into a sort of chalupa séance,
the waitress gazing out the door from another booth.

You live under a name that has never been uttered.
Hurry, ask me what I'm thinking, the waitress says to you.
I will not, you say.
And that, as you feared, was the end of it.

Hurry, ask me what I'm thinking, the waitress says to you

ACKNOWLEDGMENTS

Thanks to Steve and David,
Mia Schoen for her scans,
Normal's Books and Records of Baltimore,
and Laura Newbern.

66713793R00061